MENNO SIMONS
Dutch Anabaptist Leader

LIVING HISTORY THREADS

Menno Simons: Dutch Anabaptist Leader

ISBN 978-0-9816569-3-9

Author: Betty Yoder

Photo credits: Bethel College/Mennonite Library and Archives: 6c, 17; Kyle Brubaker: 2b, 7b; © Herald Press, Scottdale, PA, artwork by Oliver Wendell Schenk, used by permission: title page b, 2a; Emily Turner: 1, 4b, 6a, b, 9b, 10a, b, 15a, b, 21a; Dorothy Turner: 16; Wikimedia Commons/Creative Commons: BoH/7b (modified), CNG coins (http://www.cngcoins.com)/18a, b, Lokilech/3b, UM/title page a, 20a.

Cover design: Emily Turner

Cover image: © Herald Press, Scottdale, PA: artwork by Oliver Wendell Schenk, used by permission.

Facing page: Town of Pingjum in Friesland, the Netherlands, where Menno Simons first served as a priest.

Living History Threads is a history curriculum developed by Faith Builders Resource Group. For more information about Living History Threads, email fbresource@fbep.org or phone 877-222-4769.

Distributed by:
Christian Learning Resource
28500 Guys Mills Road
Guys Mills, PA 16327
www.christianlearning.org
877-222-4769

Copyright © 2010 by Faith Builders Resource Group.

Menno Simons
Dutch Anabaptist Leader

Name: Kristine

School: Fair haven

Grade: 2nd grade

Menno Simons

This is the story of Menno Simons, who lived in the Netherlands and was an important early leader of the peaceful Dutch Anabaptists.

The Netherlands in Europe

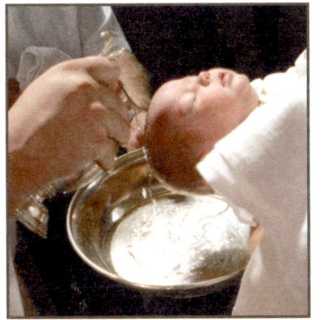

For hundreds of years, when a baby was born to almost any family in Europe, the father and mother would carry their tiny baby to the Catholic Church leaders in their area to be baptized. That way nearly everyone in Europe was part of the Catholic Church—even those who did not love Jesus or did not live a good life.

Hardly anyone read the Bible. Instead, people listened to the teachings of the church. Many of the church leaders did not read the Bible either!

A Catholic church built in 1504

In the early 1500s, some people began studying the Bible and came to believe that church members should only be those who choose to be a part of the church and who truly love Jesus and His teachings. The people who believed this started a new church.

Many others wanted to join. Soon more new churches were starting in different places.

Old water fountain in the area of these new churches

As a sign that they really wanted to follow Jesus and live a life of love, people joined this new church by being baptized. Although they had already been baptized as babies, they now asked to be baptized again, this time as grown men and women. These people also stopped taking their babies to the priests to be baptized.

Baptizing a baby

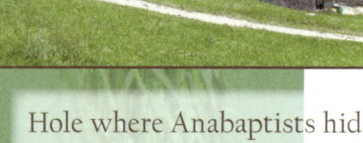

Hole where Anabaptists hid (top) in a barn (bottom)

Soldier arresting an Anabaptist lady

These were dangerous things to do! The Catholic church leaders and the government said that every baby must be baptized. The leaders started calling those who were baptized again "Anabaptists," which means "rebaptizers."

Some leaders, like Martin Luther, did not agree with the Catholics, but neither did they agree with the Anabaptists. Many church leaders were so angry that they began persecuting and killing the Anabaptists. Soon Anabaptists had to hide—or die.

The first Anabaptists lived in Switzerland. When persecution began, many Anabaptists fled to other lands. There they taught other people, and more Anabaptist churches started. Soon there were Anabaptists in the Netherlands, where Menno Simons lived.

Spread of Anabaptism

The Netherlands

Menno was born in 1496 to poor parents living in the Netherlands. Soon after he was born, his parents took him to the Catholic priest in their area to be baptized.

Windmill in the Netherlands

Village in the Netherlands

Menno made his poor parents very happy when he decided to become a priest of the Catholic Church. A priest is a preacher and church leader. As a priest Menno would be paid more money and could hope to live a more comfortable life. When he was twenty-eight years old, he took his first assignment as a priest in a village close to Witmarsum.

A priest

Church where Menno first served as priest

Even though Menno had been trained and ordained as a priest, he had never studied the Bible itself. Now that he had his own church to lead, he still didn't study the Bible. Instead he spent his time living a carefree life.

Door of the church where Menno was first a priest

Village where Menno was first a priest

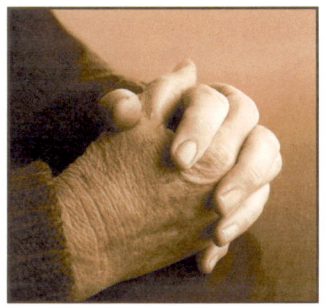

As time went on, strange things started happening to Menno. One day in the middle of a church service he suddenly wondered if what he was telling the people was really true. The thought scared him.

Menno tried to make his questions go away by praying and confessing, but he couldn't get rid of his deep doubts. After struggling with these questions for two miserable years, he began, for the first time, to study the Bible.

Studying the Bible showed Menno Simons that the Catholic Church was teaching some wrong things. So Menno started preaching differently, but he did not want to leave the Church and lose his good job.

Old Bible

Later Menno Simons heard of a man named Sicke Snyder who had been killed for being baptized a second time. "Why would anyone be willing to die for that?" Menno wondered. He liked his comfortable life.

In the next months he heard again and again of Anabaptists who refused to fight against their enemies but instead let themselves be burned, drowned, or beheaded for their beliefs.

Then Menno's own brother Peter became an Anabaptist! But Peter joined a group who chose to fight back instead of loving their enemies. One day Menno heard that his brother had been killed while fighting.

Anabaptists being burned

Menno was shocked by his brother's death. Desperate for answers to his deep questions, Menno studied the Bible more, sometimes all night long. What did the Bible teach about baptism?

Nowhere in Scripture could Menno find anything about baptizing babies. Instead, he read about people *asking* to be baptized. Now Menno had another important question: Should he stay with the Church, or obey the Bible? If he left the Catholic Church, he would lose his job and be persecuted. What would he choose?

In 1535, deeply convicted of his own sin and his need of Jesus as Savior, Menno Simons cried out to the Lord to save him. Then he began preaching God's Word boldly from the Catholic pulpit and writing articles about the Bible. Soon he knew his life was in danger and he would have to leave Witmarsum.

The Lord's Prayer in Menno's language

1 Ws Haita dw derstu biste yne hymil.
2 Dyn name wird heiligt.
3 Dyn ryck to komme.
4 Dyn wille moet schœn opt yrtryck as yne hymil.
5 Ws deilix broe jow ws jwed.
6 In verjou ws ws schylden, as wy vejae ws schildners.
7 In lied ws naet in fersieking, din fry ws vin it qwæd.
8 Din dyn is it ryck, de macht, in de heerlickheyt yn yewicheyt.
9 So mœttet wese.

Church in Witmarsum, where Menno was serving as priest when he became saved

Menno Simons left his comfortable position as a priest in 1536, joined the Anabaptists, and went into hiding. He spent a lot of time studying the Bible, teaching, and writing many articles.

Menno taught that Christians should pattern their lives after Jesus, living in love and peace instead of hating and fighting their enemies. He never forgot his brother Peter and those Anabaptists who had chosen to fight.

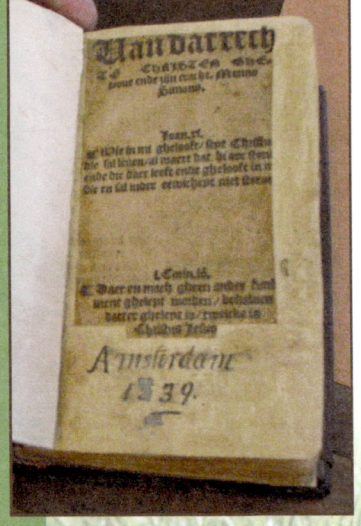

An early copy of "The True Christian Faith" by Menno Simons

Other Dutch Anabaptists began to notice what a good teacher and leader Menno Simons was. One day Menno heard a knock at the door. He thought the authorities had come to arrest him. Instead, it was Obbe Philips and some other men coming to ask Menno to be the leader of the peaceful Anabaptists in the Netherlands.

Menno Simons

As a leader, Menno Simons was in even more danger. The German emperor, Charles V, offered money to anyone who would help capture Menno. Menno had to keep moving from place to place so he would not be caught.

Coin from 1500s

The authorities tried very hard to find Menno. They could arrest anyone who helped him, talked with him, or read his books. At least two men were killed just because they gave Menno food and shelter.

Menno's wife, Gertrude, and their three children had to hide too. Menno wrote that he could not find even one little cabin where his wife and children would be safe for more than a few months.

Many times Menno traveled secretly at night to preach, baptize, and encourage other Anabaptists. Several times the authorities almost caught Menno, but he always managed to get away. Finally he and his family moved to a safer part of the country.

A castle at night

In this safe place, Menno Simons kept on writing letters and pamphlets to encourage the Anabaptists and to teach them God's ways. Because of the invention of the printing press less than one hundred years earlier, many people could have copies of Menno's writings.

House in Germany where Menno probably worked

Printing in the 1500s

Menno taught that believers should pattern their lives after Jesus. His favorite verse was I Corinthians 3:11, "For other foundation can no man lay than that is laid, which is Jesus Christ."

Memorial for Menno Simons with I Cor. 3:11 in Dutch

Menno Simons

Because Menno Simons was the main leader of the Anabaptists in the Netherlands, people began calling the Dutch Anabaptists followers of Menno, or Mennonites. Menno wished Anabaptists would just be called Christians, followers of Christ.

In 1561 Menno died a natural death and was buried in his own garden.

21

Menno Simons

Here is a famous quote from Menno Simons' writings:

> True evangelical faith
>   cannot lie dormant.
> It clothes the naked.
> It feeds the hungry.
> It comforts the sorrowful.
> It shelters the destitute.
> It serves those who harm it.
> It binds up that which is wounded.
> It has become all things to all people.